CONTENTS

D0553031

My Vacation 4

Packing for My Trip 6

V.I.P. Addresses 7

What I Know About Where I'm Going 8

Before Leaving! 9

Where... 10

The Journey There 12

Look! 14

You've Arrived 16

Some Facts About My Destination 18

What I Did 20

My New Friends 108

Souvenirs 114

Getting Around Town 116

The Best Ever 118

The Worst Ever 122

When in Rome 126

MY VACATION

Where I'm off to
_____
_____
_____

Who's going with me
_____
_____
_____

How I'm getting there
_____
_____
_____

When I'm leaving
_____
_____
_____

When I'm returning
_____
_____
_____

Space for drawing traveling companions & place where you're going

PACKING FOR MY TRIP

CLOTHES
- Belt
- Coat
- Dresses
- Fancy Pants
- Fancy Shirt
- Fancy Shoes
- Jeans
- Shorts
- Skirts
- Sneakers
- Sweaters
- Sweatshirts
- Swimsuit
- Socks
- T-Shirts
- Underwear

BATHROOM THINGS
- Comb & Brush
- Face Wash
- Hair-ties
- Toothbrush
- Toothpaste
- Soap
- Cologne

OTHER STUFF
- Address book
- Batteries
- Blanket
- Books
- Camera & Film
- CD Player/MP3
- Comics
- Games
- Hat
- Jewelry
- Money
- Passport
- Sunglasses
- Sunscreen
- Towel
- Umbrella
- Watch

OTHER STUFF
_____
_____
_____
_____

V.I.P. ADDRESSES

NAME

ADDRESS

TEL   E-MAIL

NAME

ADDRESS

TEL   E-MAIL

NAME

ADDRESS

TEL   E-MAIL

NAME

ADDRESS

TEL   E-MAIL

NAME

ADDRESS

TEL   E-MAIL

NAME

ADDRESS

TEL   E-MAIL

NAME

ADDRESS

TEL   E-MAIL

WHAT I KNOW ABOUT WHERE I'M GOING

I'm taking a vacation to
_____

because
_____
_____
_____
_____
_____
_____
_____
_____
_____
_____
_____

BEFORE LEAVING!

I wanted to learn a little bit more about where
we were going, so I decided to do some research.
I discovered the coolest stuff:

_____

_____

_____

_____

_____

_____

_____

_____

_____

_____

_____

_____

WHERE...

Draw a circle on the place you're leaving from and a star on the place you're going to.

If you're going to more than one place, draw stars on them all.
Now connect the dots!

THE JOURNEY THERE

The trip there took _____ hours.

During the trip I was soooooooooooo _____

_____

_____

_____

On our way, we passed by _____

_____

_____

_____

To occupy my time, I _____

_____

_____

_____

The best part about getting there was

The worst part about getting there was

LOOK!

Draw a picture of your journey

YOU'VE ARRIVED!

This country (or state) is bordered by

N _____

S _____

E _____

W _____

The weather here is _____

_____

_____

People speak _____

_____

_____

My first impression is _____

_____

_____

Draw a map of the country (or state)

SOME FACTS ABOUT MY DESTINATION

This place was established in
_____

The first people here were
_____

_____

Their system of government is
_____

_____

The head of the country/state is
_____

_____

Their special holiday is
_____

_____

_____

Some famous landmarks are

_____

_____

Their traditional foods are

_____

_____

_____

_____

Some unique customs are

_____

_____

_____

_____

_____

_____

DATE   PLACE

What I Did

What I Saw

Where and What I Ate

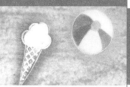

DATE   PLACE

What I Did

What I Saw

Where and What I Ate

DATE   PLACE

What I Did

_____

_____

_____

_____

What I Saw

_____

_____

_____

_____

Where and What I Ate

_____

_____

_____

DATE   PLACE

What I Did

What I Saw

Where and What I Ate

DATE   PLACE

What I Did

What I Saw

Where and What I Ate

DATE   PLACE

What I Did

What I Saw

Where and What I Ate

DATE   PLACE

What I Did

What I Saw

Where and What I Ate

DATE   PLACE

What I Did

What I Saw

Where and What I Ate

DATE   PLACE

What I Did

What I Saw

Where and What I Ate

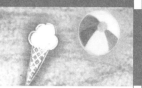

DATE   PLACE

What I Did

What I Saw

Where and What I Ate

DATE PLACE

What I Did

What I Saw

Where and What I Ate

DATE   PLACE

What I Did

What I Saw

Where and What I Ate

DATE   PLACE

What I Did

What I Saw

Where and What I Ate

DATE   PLACE

What I Did

What I Saw

Where and What I Ate

DATE   PLACE

What I Did

What I Saw

Where and What I Ate

DATE   PLACE

What I Did

What I Saw

Where and What I Ate

DATE _____ PLACE _____

What I Did

_____

_____

_____

_____

What I Saw

_____

_____

_____

_____

Where and What I Ate

_____

_____

_____

DATE   PLACE

What I Did

What I Saw

Where and What I Ate

DATE _____ **PLACE** _____

What I Did
_____
_____
_____
_____
_____

What I Saw
_____
_____
_____
_____
_____

Where and What I Ate
_____
_____
_____
_____

DATE   PLACE

What I Did

What I Saw

Where and What I Ate

DATE   PLACE

What I Did

What I Saw

Where and What I Ate

DATE   PLACE

What I Did

_____

_____

_____

_____

What I Saw

_____

_____

_____

_____

Where and What I Ate

_____

_____

_____

DATE

PLACE

What I Did

What I Saw

Where and What I Ate

DATE _____ PLACE _____

What I Did
_____
_____
_____
_____

What I Saw
_____
_____
_____
_____

Where and What I Ate
_____
_____
_____
_____

DATE   **PLACE**

What I Did

What I Saw

Where and What I Ate

DATE   PLACE

What I Did

_____

_____

_____

_____

What I Saw

_____

_____

_____

_____

Where and What I Ate

_____

_____

_____

_____

DATE

PLACE

What I Did

What I Saw

Where and What I Ate

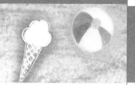

DATE **PLACE**

What I Did

What I Saw

Where and What I Ate

DATE

PLACE

What I Did

What I Saw

Where and What I Ate

DATE   PLACE

What I Did

What I Saw

Where and What I Ate

DATE

PLACE

What I Did

What I Saw

Where and What I Ate

DATE   PLACE

What I Did

What I Saw

Where and What I Ate

DATE _____ **PLACE** _____

What I Did
_____
_____
_____
_____

What I Saw
_____
_____
_____
_____

Where and What I Ate
_____
_____
_____

DATE   PLACE

What I Did

What I Saw

Where and What I Ate

DATE   PLACE

What I Did

What I Saw

Where and What I Ate

DATE _____ PLACE _____

What I Did
_____
_____
_____
_____

What I Saw
_____
_____
_____
_____

Where and What I Ate
_____
_____
_____

DATE

PLACE

What I Did

What I Saw

Where and What I Ate

DATE   PLACE

What I Did

What I Saw

Where and What I Ate

DATE

PLACE

What I Did

What I Saw

Where and What I Ate

DATE   **PLACE**

What I Did

What I Saw

Where and What I Ate

DATE _____ PLACE _____

What I Did _____

_____

_____

_____

_____

What I Saw _____

_____

_____

_____

_____

Where and What I Ate _____

_____

_____

_____

DATE   PLACE

What I Did

_____

_____

_____

_____

What I Saw

_____

_____

_____

_____

Where and What I Ate

_____

_____

_____

DATE   PLACE

What I Did

What I Saw

Where and What I Ate

DATE   PLACE

What I Did

What I Saw

Where and What I Ate

DATE   PLACE

What I Did

_____

_____

_____

_____

What I Saw

_____

_____

_____

_____

Where and What I Ate

_____

_____

_____

_____

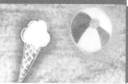

DATE   **PLACE**

What I Did

What I Saw

Where and What I Ate

DATE   PLACE

What I Did

What I Saw

Where and What I Ate

DATE   PLACE

What I Did

What I Saw

Where and What I Ate

DATE _____ PLACE _____

What I Did _____

_____

_____

_____

What I Saw _____

_____

_____

_____

_____

Where and What I Ate _____

_____

_____

_____

DATE   PLACE

What I Did

What I Saw

Where and What I Ate

DATE _____ **PLACE** _____

What I Did
_____
_____
_____
_____

What I Saw
_____
_____
_____
_____

Where and What I Ate
_____
_____
_____

DATE   PLACE

What I Did

What I Saw

Where and What I Ate

DATE _____ PLACE _____

What I Did
_____

_____

_____

_____

What I Saw
_____

_____

_____

_____

Where and What I Ate
_____

_____

_____

_____

DATE _____ PLACE _____

What I Did
_____
_____
_____
_____

What I Saw
_____
_____
_____
_____

Where and What I Ate
_____
_____
_____
_____

DATE   PLACE

What I Did

What I Saw

Where and What I Ate

DATE   PLACE

What I Did

What I Saw

Where and What I Ate

DATE   PLACE

What I Did

What I Saw

Where and What I Ate

DATE   PLACE

What I Did

What I Saw

Where and What I Ate

DATE _____ **PLACE** _____

What I Did _____

_____

_____

_____

What I Saw _____

_____

_____

_____

_____

Where and What I Ate _____

_____

_____

_____

DATE   PLACE

What I Did

What I Saw

Where and What I Ate

DATE   PLACE

What I Did

What I Saw

Where and What I Ate

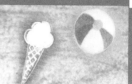

DATE   PLACE

What I Did

What I Saw

Where and What I Ate

DATE

PLACE

What I Did

What I Saw

Where and What I Ate

DATE   PLACE

What I Did

What I Saw

Where and What I Ate

DATE _____ PLACE _____

What I Did
_____
_____
_____
_____

What I Saw
_____
_____
_____
_____

Where and What I Ate
_____
_____
_____

DATE   PLACE

What I Did

What I Saw

Where and What I Ate

DATE   PLACE

What I Did

What I Saw

Where and What I Ate

DATE   **PLACE**

What I Did

What I Saw

Where and What I Ate

DATE   PLACE

What I Did

What I Saw

Where and What I Ate

DATE _____ PLACE _____

What I Did _____
_____
_____
_____
_____

What I Saw _____
_____
_____
_____
_____

Where and What I Ate _____
_____
_____
_____

DATE   PLACE

What I Did

What I Saw

Where and What I Ate

DATE **PLACE**

What I Did

What I Saw

Where and What I Ate

DATE   PLACE

What I Did

What I Saw

Where and What I Ate

DATE   PLACE
_____

What I Did
_____

_____

_____

_____

What I Saw
_____

_____

_____

_____

Where and What I Ate
_____

_____

_____

_____

DATE   PLACE

What I Did

What I Saw

Where and What I Ate

DATE

PLACE

What I Did

What I Saw

Where and What I Ate

DATE   PLACE

What I Did

What I Saw

Where and What I Ate

DATE   PLACE

What I Did

What I Saw

Where and What I Ate

DATE   PLACE

What I Did

What I Saw

Where and What I Ate

DATE   **PLACE**

What I Did

What I Saw

Where and What I Ate

DATE   PLACE

What I Did

What I Saw

Where and What I Ate

DATE   PLACE

What I Did

What I Saw

Where and What I Ate

DATE

PLACE

What I Did

What I Saw

Where and What I Ate

DATE   PLACE

What I Did

What I Saw

Where and What I Ate

Here's some more space for you to doodle, draw and write!

Use this space to doodle, draw a picture and write down some thoughts about your vacation

MY NEW FRIENDS

Name

How I Met My Friend

What We Did Together

Address

Phone Number

e-mail

Name

How I Met My Friend

What We Did Together

Address

Phone Number

e-mail

Paste photos or use this space to draw pictures of your new friends!

MY NEW FRIENDS

Name

How I Met My Friend

What We Did Together

Address

Phone Number

e-mail

Name

How I Met My Friend

What We Did Together

Address

Phone Number

e-mail

Paste photos or use this space to draw pictures of your new friends!

MY NEW FRIENDS

Name

How I Met My Friend

What We Did Together

Address

Phone Number

e-mail

Name

How I Met My Friend

What We Did Together

Address

Phone Number

e-mail

Paste photos or use this space to draw pictures of your new friends!

SOUVENIRS

For	Souvenir

SOUVENIRS

For   Souvenir

GETTING AROUND TOWN

While traveling, I rode

A **BICYCLE**

A **BOAT**

A **BUS**

A **CAMEL**

A **CAR**

A **GONDOLA**

A **METRO**

A **RICKSHAW**

A **SUBWAY**

A **TAXI**

A **TRAIN**

A **TROLLEY**

Draw a picture of you getting around town!

THE BEST EVER

ROOM TO DRAW

THE WORST EVER

ROOM TO DRAW

WHEN IN ROME

(Few Handy Words to Know) . . .

ENGLISH	SPANISH	FRENCH
Hello	Hola	Bonjour
Good-bye	Adiós	Au revoir
Please	Por favor	S'il vous plaît
Thank you	Gracias	Merci
You're welcome	De nada	De rien
Excuse me	Discúlpeme	Excusez-moi
How much does it cost?	Cuanto cuesta?	Combien ça coûte?
Where's the restroom?	Donde está el baño?	Ou sont les toilettes?

ITALIAN	GERMAN
Ciao	Hallo
Arrivederci	Auf Wiedersehen
Favore	Bitte
Grazie	Danke
Siete Benvenuto	Bitte
Scusa	Entschuldigen Sie
Cuánto costa?	Wieviel kostet das?
Dov'è il gabinetto?	Wo ist hier die Toilette?

Illustration: Sarah Hollander
Text: Kristen Pollak
Design: Lorena Siminovich

Design © Galison

Manufactured in China
ISBN 978-0-7353-1505-1

Please visit us at
www.mudpuppy.com